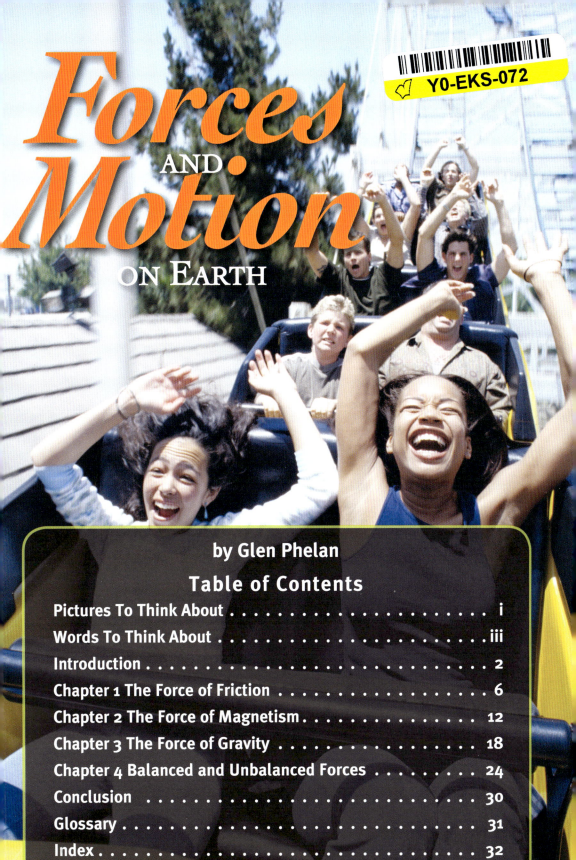

Forces AND Motion ON EARTH

by Glen Phelan

Table of Contents

Pictures To Think About

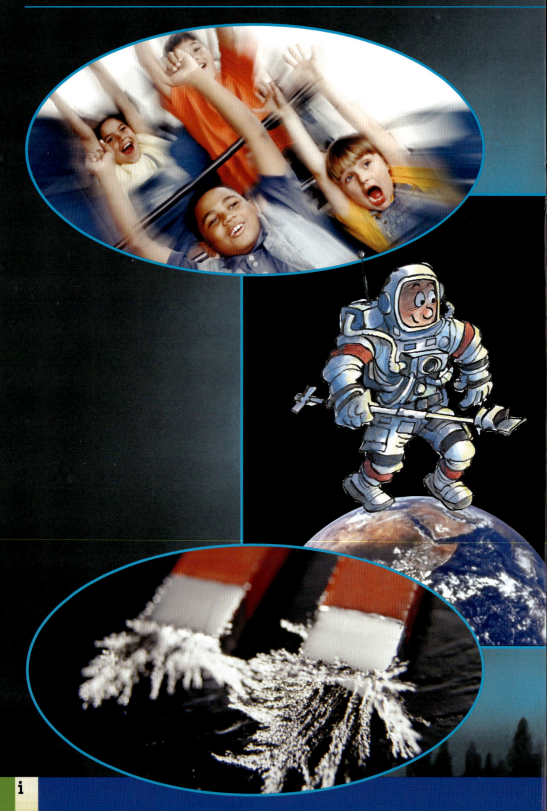

Words To Think About

Characteristics

- a force
- happens when things rub together
- ?

friction

What do you think the word **friction** means?

Examples

- tire pressing against road
- pencil writing on paper
- ?

gravity

What do you think the word **gravity** means?

Latin:
gravis
(heavy)

Latin:
-ity
(degree of)

mass

What do you think the word **mass** means in this book?

Meaning 1
amount of matter in an object (noun)

Meaning 2
large group of people (noun)

Meaning 3
main part of something (noun)

Introduction

"**K**eep your balance," you tell yourself. You crouch low on your skateboard. You begin to roll downhill. Faster and faster you go. The wind is blowing hard in your face now. Will you make it up the other side of the ramp? Yes!

What a wild ride! What a fun way to explore the science of **motion** (MOH-shun). Motion is any change in an object's position. You may not be a skateboarder, but you make different motions every day. When you raise your hand in class, you move it. That is a motion. When a flag waves in the wind, it changes position. That is also a motion.

Look around you on your way home from school. You might notice a hundred things moving. Why do they move? How do they move?

◀ Raising your arms is an everyday motion, as is a flag blowing in the wind. ▼

▲ A skateboarder is in constant motion.

It's All About Forces

Think about flying a kite. You hold the kite up with one hand. You grab the string with the other hand. You run and let go of the kite. The kite moves higher and higher. Up in the sky, the kite dives and climbs. It spins in circles. What causes all those motions?

Motion is caused by **force**. A force is a push or a pull. Whenever you see something moving, or motion, you know that pushes and pulls are at work.

▲ **Forces—pushes and pulls—make the kite move.**

Forces make objects move. Forces make objects speed up and slow down. Forces also make things change direction and stop.

Suppose you give a soccer ball a kick. The kick is a push, or a force. The kick makes the ball roll across the grass. Then other forces make the ball slow down and stop.

We experience many forces every day on the planet Earth. Read on to learn more about these forces.

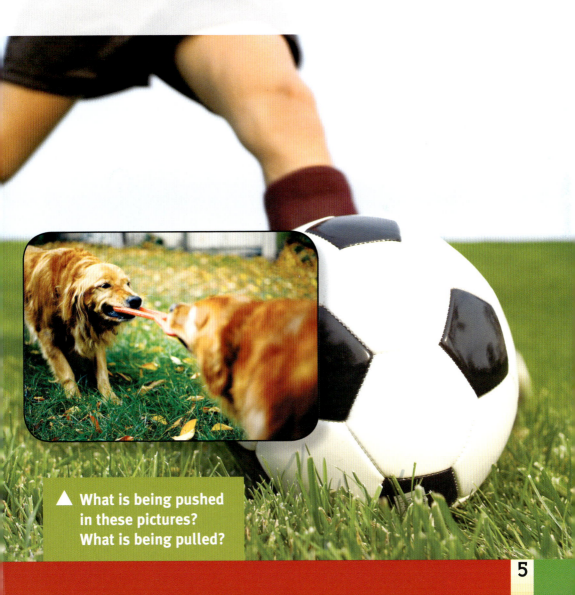

▲ What is being pushed in these pictures? What is being pulled?

The Force of Friction

*T*HUMP! The BMX bike lands hard at the bottom of the dirt hill. The racer keeps her balance. She pedals up the next hill and zooms over the top. Will she make the sharp curve at the bottom?

She lands with a bang. She leans to the left. The tires press against the ground and kick up a cloud of dirt. The bike leaves deep tire tracks in the ground.

Why didn't the wheels slide out from under the bike at the sharp turn? The answer is **friction** (FRIK-shun). Friction is a force that exists when one object rubs against another object.

Friction ▶ between the tires and the ground keeps the bike on the track but sends the dirt flying.

When two objects rub against each other, they are actually pushing against each other. This pushing creates friction. Friction keeps objects from sliding past each other easily.

What if the BMX racer were riding on ice? What would happen at the sharp turn? You are right—it would be a wipeout! The bike would slide like a hockey puck. That is because smooth surfaces, such as ice, produce less friction than rough surfaces, such as the dirt trail.

It's a Fact

Friction is produced when uneven spots and jagged edges rub against and get caught on each other. No object or surface is perfectly smooth. Even a piece of highly polished metal is rough when seen under a microscope.

Friction All Around

You can see friction at work all around you. When you walk, you push off and step forward. Friction is produced between the soles of your shoes and the ground. Friction keeps you from slipping.

Are you sitting in a chair? Friction keeps you from sliding off. When you write with a pencil, friction makes some of the pencil lead rub off onto the paper. When things are rubbing, or even just touching, friction is acting between them.

▼ **You use friction in many ways to ride a bike.**

Pedal Power

How do you use friction on a bike? Hop on to find out.

1. You push against the pedals. That moves the wheels.
2. The wheels push against the ground. You roll forward.
3. The rubber grips increase friction with your hands.
4. You squeeze the hand brakes. This makes the brake pads rub against the wheel.
5. Friction between the brake pads and the wheel slows the bike.

Friction between you and the air also slows you down. This friction is called **air resistance** (AIR reh-ZIS-tens). As you move, air particles push against you. You have to keep pedaling to overcome air resistance and friction between the tires and the pavement.

It's a Fact

Air resistance, like any other friction, produces heat. It's not enough heat to feel when you ride a bike. But when the space shuttle re-enters Earth's atmosphere, the heat from air resistance is so great that the shuttle glows.

More Friction—or Less?

Sometimes you want to increase friction. Suppose you go rock climbing. You wear rubber-soled shoes. That is because they provide more friction than smooth-soled shoes. That allows you to grip the rocks better.

Sometimes you want to reduce, or make less, friction. That is what oil does in a car's engine. The engine has dozens of moving parts. Many of them rub together very quickly. The friction between the parts can wear them down. The friction also produces a lot of heat. That heat can ruin the engine. Oil reduces friction. Oil lets the moving parts slide more easily against one another.

▲ **Rubber-soled shoes grip better than smooth-soled shoes.**

Imagine

Suppose friction was suddenly "turned off" for an hour. How would it affect motion? How would it affect what you're doing right now?

Hands-On Experiment
How Ball Bearings Work

Small metal balls called ball bearings help reduce friction between two surfaces. How do they work?

What You'll Need
- 2 identical pie plates
- 10–20 marbles

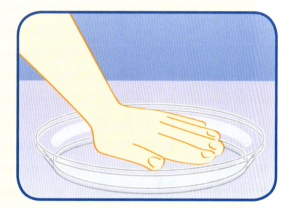

What To Do
1. Set one pie plate inside the other. Try to spin the top plate.
2. Remove the top plate. Put the marbles in the bottom plate.
3. Set the other plate on top of the marbles. Try to spin the top plate.

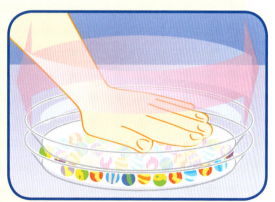

What Do You Think?
1. How did the marbles change the force needed to overcome friction?
2. Think of two examples where ball bearings would be useful.

CHAPTER 2

The Force of Magnetism

The night is clear and dark. You look up at the sky to admire the stars. Suddenly, a curtain of red, blue, and green light begins to glow before your eyes. This beautiful light show takes place in the far northern and southern parts of Earth. In the north, it is called the northern lights, or aurora borealis (uh-ROR-uh bor-ee-A-lis). In the south, it is called aurora australis.

What causes an aurora? It is the same force that holds papers on your refrigerator—**magnetism**.

The northern lights are caused by magnetism. ▶

Magnetism is a force. Magnetism attracts, or pulls on, things that contain iron. An object that has magnetism is called a **magnet**.

▲ Bits of iron gather at the poles, where magnetism is strongest.

Every magnet has two poles, or ends. One pole is called the north pole. The other pole is called the south pole.

The force of magnetism is strongest near the poles of a magnet. You can see that in the picture. This magnet was placed near tiny bits of iron. The magnet pulled on the iron bits to create the pattern shown. Where did most of the iron bits go?

Magnetic Fields

Suppose you place a magnet at one end of a table and a paper clip at the other end. The magnet should attract the paper clip because paper clips are made of steel and steel is made from iron.

In this case, the paper clip doesn't move. Why? The paper clip is outside the magnet's **magnetic field** (mag-NEH-tik FEELD). A magnetic field is the area around a magnet where its magnetism acts.

Large, powerful magnets have large magnetic fields. Smaller, weaker magnets have smaller magnetic fields.

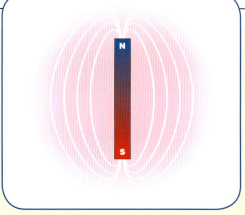

▲ **Every magnet has two poles. A magnetic field surrounds a magnet.**

▲ **Earth has two poles, the North Pole and the South Pole.**

 point **Think About It**

Compare the diagram on this page with the picture on page 13. Can you tell where the magnetic field is in the picture?

Everyday Science

Magnets are all around. You probably have some on your refrigerator that are holding up notes. But did you know that magnets are inside your refrigerator, too? Motors that run refrigerators, vacuum cleaners, and other machines use magnets.

Hands-on Experiment

What things in your home or school contain iron? Get a magnet and find out what objects are attracted to it. (Remember, steel has iron in it.) Use the items listed here, record your findings in the table, and compare your results with those of your classmates.

Item	Contains Iron?	
	Yes	No
Quarter	☐	☐
Dime	☐	☐
Nickel	☐	☐
Penny	☐	☐
Spoon	☐	☐
Fork	☐	☐
DoorKnob	☐	☐
Key	☐	☐

Earth is a huge magnet. Earth has magnetic north and south poles. If you get lost, you can use a compass to find your way. The compass needle is a magnet. It always points to Earth's magnetic north pole. Once you know where magnetic north is, you can figure out other directions.

Earth also has a huge magnetic field around it. Tiny particles from the sun travel through space. When the particles reach Earth's magnetic field, they get pulled toward the poles. The particles then hit gas particles in Earth's atmosphere. This gives off light. That is what makes auroras.

▲ A compass works because Earth is a huge magnet.

Hands-on Experiment

Make A Compass

It's easy to make a compass. All you need is a magnet and a way to let it move freely.

What You'll Need

- bar magnet • cork • bowl of water • masking tape

What To Do

1. Tape the magnet to the top of the cork.
2. Carefully place the cork into the bowl of water so that the cork floats. Make sure the magnet doesn't get wet.
3. Let the cork turn in the water until it comes to a stop. Note which end of the magnet points north. If you don't know which way is north, ask your teacher or an adult.
4. Take the cork out of the water. Stick a piece of masking tape on the end of the magnet that pointed north.
5. Place the cork back in the water. See if the magnet points north again.

What do you think?

1. How is this compass like a compass you can buy?
2. How could you make a compass without using water?

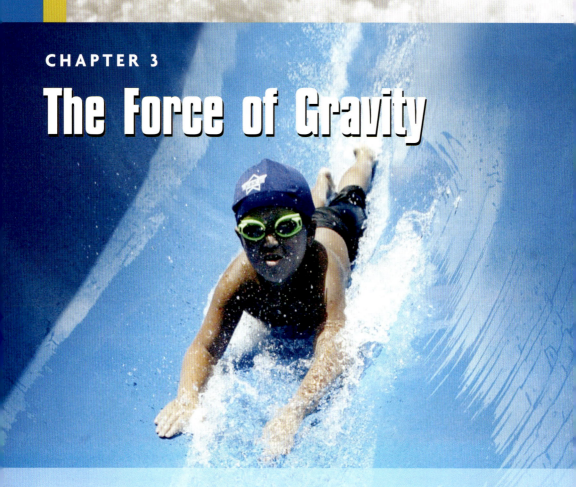

CHAPTER 3
The Force of Gravity

Nothing beats the summer heat like a cool waterslide. You climb to the top. You push off. You let out a loud yell. Down you go. Why down? **Gravity** (GRA-vih-tee) is pulling you down.

Gravity is a force that pulls any two objects together. For example, a pencil falls because Earth is pulling the pencil toward it. This pulling force is gravity.

▲ The force of Earth's gravity pulls you down the slide.

Gravity can be so weak that you cannot feel it. Or gravity can be so strong that you cannot escape it. The gravity of an object depends on the object's **mass**. Mass is the amount of matter, or material, an object is made of. The greater the mass of an object, the stronger the pull of gravity.

Think of the falling pencil again. You drop a pencil. Earth pulls on the pencil as it falls. Remember that gravity acts between any two objects. Your body is also pulling on the pencil. Earth has a lot more mass than you do. That is why its pull is a lot stronger. The pencil falls toward Earth, not toward you.

It's a Fact

When Earth pulls on a falling pencil, the pencil pulls on Earth with the same amount of force. Then why doesn't Earth rise toward the pencil? Actually, it does! But the motion is too small to notice.

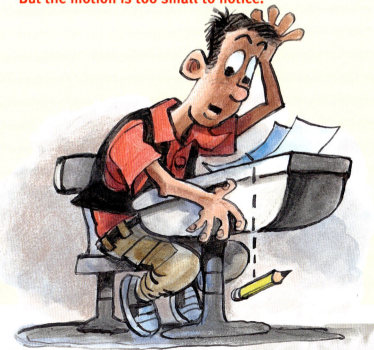

◀ When an object falls, it is being pulled by the force of gravity.

Gravity and Weight

"How much do I weigh?" you wonder. You step on a scale. It may surprise you to know that you are really finding out how much Earth's gravity is pulling on you. **Weight** is a measure of the pull of gravity on an object.

Now suppose you put a kitten on the scale. The kitten weighs much less than you do. Why? The kitten has less mass than you do. The Earth pulls on the kitten with less force, and so the kitten weighs less.

1. Solve This

Most people in the United States and the United Kingdom measure weight in pounds. But scientists measure weight in newtons (N). A medium-sized apple is 1 newton, or about 0.2 pounds. If you cut an apple in four equal slices, about how much would each slice weigh in newtons?

Weight and Mass

Weight and mass are related, but they are not the same. To see how they are different, let's visit the moon.

The moon is smaller than Earth and has less mass. The force of gravity on the moon is less than on Earth. In fact, the moon's gravity is only about one-sixth of Earth's gravity. That means the moon pulls on an object with only one-sixth the force that Earth would pull on it. So an astronaut who weighs 160 pounds on Earth

2. Solve This

Suppose astronauts collected a rock that weighed half a pound on the moon. How much did it weigh when they got back to Earth?

would weigh one-sixth of that (about 27 pounds) on the moon. The astronaut weighs less but his mass does not change. He is still the same size. He still has the same amount of matter.

Which Falls Faster?

You hold a bowling ball at your waist. A friend holds a volleyball at the same height. The balls are about the same size. You both let go of the balls at the same time. Which one hits the ground first?

The bowling ball is much heavier than the volleyball. It has much more mass. The bowling ball falls faster and hits the ground first, right? Wrong! Gravity makes all objects fall with the same speed as long as no other forces affect the objects. The bowling ball and the volleyball hit the ground at the same time.

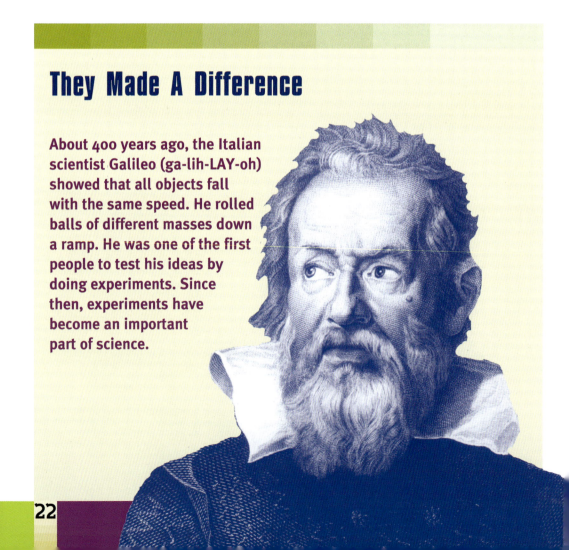

They Made A Difference

About 400 years ago, the Italian scientist Galileo (ga-lih-LAY-oh) showed that all objects fall with the same speed. He rolled balls of different masses down a ramp. He was one of the first people to test his ideas by doing experiments. Since then, experiments have become an important part of science.

What if you drop a feather and a bowling ball at the same time? Will they hit the ground together? You probably know the answer. The ball drops quickly while the feather drifts down slowly. That's because other forces besides gravity affect the objects. Air resistance, for example, slows the feather more than it slows the ball.

What if there were no air? Then the feather and ball should fall at the same speed. In 1971, an astronaut named David Scott did an experiment to prove that idea. On the airless moon, he dropped a feather and a hammer. The feather and the hammer hit the moon's surface at the same time.

Hands-on Experiment

See for yourself how gravity makes objects fall at the same speed. Get two objects that have close to the same shape and size, but are different weights. You might use two kinds of coins or two kinds of balls. Hold the objects up and let them go at the same time. Watch what happens.

CHAPTER 4

Balanced and Unbalanced Forces

R eady, set, pull!" The tug-of-war begins. Both teams are pulling with all their might. Still, no one is moving closer to the line. Both teams are pulling with the same amount of force and in opposite directions. The forces are equal, or balanced. When **balanced forces** (BA-lunst FORS-ez) act on an object, the object does not move.

What happens if one team pulls with more force than the other team? The forces are now unequal and unbalanced. The teams and the rope move in the direction of the stronger pull. When **unbalanced forces** (un-BA-lunst FORS-ez) act on an object, the object moves or changes its motion.

Everything around you involves balanced and unbalanced forces. For example, hold this book up while you read. The upward force of your hands balances the downward force of gravity. The forces are balanced, so the book

doesn't move. Now lower the book. You are not pushing up with as much force. Gravity still pulls down with the same amount of force as before. The forces are now unbalanced, and so the book moves down.

3. Solve This

In a tug-of-war, Team A pulls with a force of 1,250 N. Team B pulls with a force of 1,585 N. Which team wins? How much more force does the winning team pull with?

Combining Forces

Most objects have many forces acting on them at the same time. Here are some of the forces acting on you when you move a wheelbarrow.

1. You pull up on the handles.
2. You push against the ground with your feet.
3. Friction acts between your shoes and the ground.
4. Friction acts between the wheel and the ground.
5. The wind pushes you to one side.
6. You push back against the wind.
7. Gravity is constantly pulling you and the wheelbarrow down.

What forces ▶ are acting on the man and the wheelbarrow?

With all these forces pushing and pulling at you, how do you get anywhere? The answer is that the forces combine. When the forces combine, sometimes they cancel each other out. The amount of force that remains causes motion.

Take a look at the photo below. You can almost feel the pushes and pulls of the raging water. The people also push and pull with their paddles to avoid dangerous rocks. What other forces are acting on the raft?

point

Talk About It
Think of an action that you did today. Turn to a partner and describe the different forces that acted on you.

▲ Rafters push and pull to fight the forces of the rushing water.

The direction of a force is just as important as the amount of force. Suppose you and a friend want to move a heavy snowball. Does it make sense to push in opposite directions? No, you would push in the same direction. When your forces work together, it is easier to move the snowball.

▲ It is easier to push a big snowball if you combine forces.

Careers in Science

Do you enjoy building models and making things? Do you like to take things apart and figure out how they work? Then civil engineering (SIH-vul en-juh-NEER-ing) might be the career for you. Civil engineers design bridges, dams, roads, and other structures. Civil engineers must understand all the forces that act on structures in order to build them safely. To become a civil engineer, you have to study science and math and earn a college degree in engineering. As a civil engineer, you might work for the government, a private company, or start your own engineering company.

Conclusion

Every move you make is caused by one or more forces. Among these forces are friction, magnetism, and gravity. Friction happens when one object rubs against another object. Magnetism is a force that attracts things made of iron. Gravity is a force that pulls any two objects together.

Usually, more than one force acts on an object at a time. If the forces are balanced, the object will not move. The object only moves when the forces are unbalanced.

Now that you know more about forces, use the concept map shown here to help explain the pictures on pages 4–5 and 16.

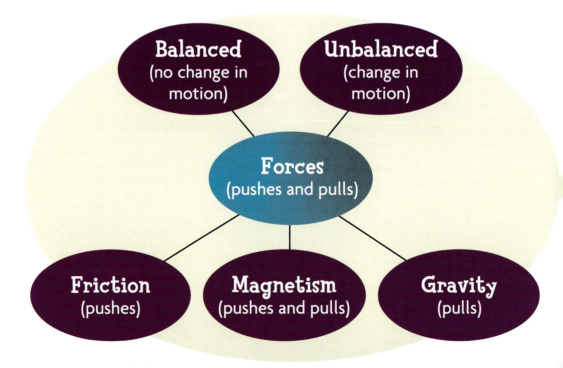

Balanced (no change in motion)

Unbalanced (change in motion)

Forces (pushes and pulls)

Friction (pushes)

Magnetism (pushes and pulls)

Gravity (pulls)

Glossary

air resistance	(AIR reh-ZIS-tens) friction between an object and the air (page 9)
balanced forces	(BA-lunst FORS-ez) forces that act equally on an object but in opposite directions (page 24)
force	(FORS) a push or a pull (page 4)
friction	(FRIK-shun) a force that happens when one object rubs against another object (page 6)
gravity	(GRA-vih-tee) a force that pulls any two objects together (page 18)
magnet	(MAG-net) an object that has magnetism (page 13)
magnetic field	(mag-NEH-tik FEELD) the area around a magnet where its magnetism acts (page 14)
magnetism	(MAG-neh-tih-zum) a force that attracts things made of iron (page 12)
mass	(MAS) the amount of matter, or material, an object is made of (page 19)
motion	(MOH-shun) any change in an object's position (page 2)
unbalanced forces	(un-BA-lunst FORS-ez) forces that result in an object moving or changing its motion (page 24)
weight	(WATE) a measure of the pull of gravity on an object (page 20)

Solve This Answers

----

1. **Page 20:** .25 N
2. **Page 21:** 3 pounds
3. **Page 25:** Team B wins; 335 N

Index